THE MYSTERY BOX

Monty Edwards

First published by Making Magic Happen Academy, 2017

Copyright © 2017 Monty Edwards
Cover design and illustrations by Veronica Rooke

All rights reserved. No part of this book may be used or reproduced by any means, graphic, electronic, or mechanical, including photocopying, recording, taping or by any information storage retrieval system without the written permission of the copyright owner except in the case of brief quotations embodied in critical articles and reviews.
This is a work of fiction. Names, characters, businesses, places, events and incidents are either the products of the author'/s' imagination or used in a fictitious manner. Any resemblance to actual persons, living or dead, or actual events is purely coincidental.

National Library of Australia
Cataloguing-in-Publication data:
Mystery Box, The/ Monty Edwards

ISBN: (sc) 978-0-6481284-6-5
ISBN: (e) 978-0-6481284-7-2
Juvenile Fiction/ Poetry

Making Magic Happen Academy books may be ordered through online booksellers or by contacting:
www.makingmagichappenacademy.com

The Mystery Box
Contents

Animals & Birds	Super Swimmer	2
	The Three Bears Retold	2
	A Zooish Riddle	4
	High Tea	5
	Words for Birds	6
	Alphabetical Animals	8
	Squirrel Sightings	9
Garden Creatures	Rainbow's End	12
	Small Wonder	13
	The Tortoise	13
	Supersnail	14
	The Happy Cricket	15
	Who's Home?	16
Food & Family	The Mystery Box	18
	Sweet Treats	19
	A Happiness Recipe	20
	Beating Eric's Eating	21
	Sharing the Secret	23
	Tongue Torture	24

People & Places	The Mail Tin	26
	Beach Bottle	27
	My Ride to School	28
	Pathway in the Park	29
	Holiday Playground	32
	Clown Caper	33
	My Secret Place	34
	Buccaneer Secrets	35
	Colours of Courage	37
	Beach Cones	38
Play Time	My Tall Tower	40
	Bubble Trouble	41
	Train Lines	42
	Space Traveller	42
	Seeking Stardom	44
	Wally's Folly	45
	Rubik Remembered	46
Weather Watching	Stop, rain, stop!	48
	Winter: A Child's Guide	49
	Winter Picnic	50
	Sometimes . . .	52
Fun With Words	T is for Trouble	54
	Party Preparation	55
	Ready to Rhyme	55
	Wacky Words	56
	A Reason to Rhyme	57
Acknowledgements		58
About the author		59

Foreword

*I have come to know Monty's poetry well through my role
as editor of the Australian Children's Poetry site
(www.australianchildrenspoetry.com)
founded by Dianne Bates.
Monty is a frequent contributor to the Poem of the Day
blog on the site, enthusiastically embracing the weekly
poetry prompts. It is always a pleasure to receive
his submissions.
They are always child friendly and well crafted, and often
bring a smile to my day. Monty is a versatile poet who can
deliver humour from the everyday and gentle insights to
provoke deeper thinking. He has a wonderful capacity to
see the world from a child's perspective. I am delighted this
collection will take his poetry to a wider audience of
young readers who I am sure will enjoy it as much as
the child in me.*

*Teena Raffa-Mulligan
Children's author and poet.*

ANIMALS & BIRDS

Super Swimmer

Sammy the seal loves to swim in the sea.
He eats fish for breakfast and eats fish for tea.
He doesn't much mind all their bones and their scales,
For he swallows them whole from their heads to their tails.
Then once he is full he is ready to rest
And a rock in the sun is the spot he likes best.

When Sammy is swimming a shark may glide past
And that's time for Sammy to move very fast!
For Sammy is smart and has more than a hunch
That a shark thinks a seal makes a rather nice lunch!
Since sharks have sharp teeth like the points on a saw,
They're clearly a threat that no seal can ignore.

If sometimes you find him asleep on a beach,
Make sure that you keep yourself out of his reach,
For if you should rouse him and give him a fright
He may be upset and get ready to fight.
So better by far that you give him no cause,
Since though without fists, he has very strong jaws!

The Three Bears Retold

There once was a family named Bear
Who thought they had nothing to wear.
While eating their oats
They remembered their coats
And decided to go to the fair.

The number of Bears you would see
Was just a small family of three.
There was Mother and Dad
With a Baby they had
And they lived in a house near a tree.

They went to the fair to have fun,
But their time there had hardly begun
When they each said: "I'm hot!"
For it seems they forgot
That their fur coats held heat in the sun.

"We'd better go home," they all said.
"Let's finish our porridge instead."
(If only they knew
A young girl was there too,
Who was sleeping in Baby Bear's bed)!

As soon as they opened the door,
They saw that their bowls had held more.
Some porridge not there!
One broken small chair!
But a bigger surprise was in store.

For then the whole family Bear
Were wanting to search everywhere.
When they saw Baby's bed
Held a young girl instead
They growled: "That is really unfair!"

Their guest got straight up with a shock.
(The Bears had neglected to knock).
She ran out the door
And they saw her no more
While the Bears quickly fitted a lock!

*A Zooish Riddle**

Today I'm all excited
'cause we're going to the zoo
And there's something that we'll see there
that I'll now describe to you.
Since it's found throughout Australia
you would hardly call it rare -
Live for long in any city
and you'll surely find one there.

Not so common in the country,
but you still may see a few,
It's no cuddly koala
nor a bounding kangaroo.
Do not think of an echidna
or a little bandicoot;
This is something that you'll
never ever hear described as cute.

In appearance, on occasions,
it's been likened to a snake,
But it's certainly not legless
in the moves that it can make.
If you see a very large one,
you will wish it wasn't so.
Should it move along quite slowly,
you may even see it grow!

You can rule out any reptile,
bird or fish that comes to mind,
But I will not tease you further:
that would really be unkind.
It's a line. No, not a lion.
There, I've given you a clue.
It's a line of ticket buyers
gaining entry through a queue!

* *First published in The School Magazine: Blast Off. June 2017.*

High Tea

When pelicans are flying low,
With open beaks they say "Hello"
To any fish they gladly see
That could provide a tasty tea,
For like a furry flippered seal,
They do enjoy a fishy meal.

So after taking time to greet,
These hungry birds prepare to eat,
(While under beaks, there hangs a store
For extra, should they want some more).
Then up they rise to sail the sky:
Their beaks too full to say "Goodbye"!

Words for Birds

I have a cockatoo named Bert.
I'm teaching him to talk.
For years the best that he could do
was simply screech and squawk.
He made the most unpleasant sounds
- I had to walk away.
I wondered which words would be best
to get my Bert to say.

"A dictionary might help," I thought,
but that was clearly wrong:
To read right through a dictionary
would take me far too long!
In any case, some words I found,
I didn't want to use,
Since words I couldn't say myself
were not the ones to choose!

My teacher knows a lot of words,
but when I went to ask
What she'd suggest to be some words
for such a tricky task,
The teacher only shook her head.
"I really wouldn't know," she said.
That night before I went to bed,
I thought to ask my Dad instead.

My Dad said: "Why not ask your Mum?
If you want words, then she's the one!"
So off I went to find my Mum,
but words for birds? She gave me none.
Mum said: "Now son, it's getting late.
It's time for bed!" Those words I hate.
It seemed I must accept my fate.
To get her help I'd have to wait.

I went to bed. What could I do?
I hoped that sleep might bring a clue.
A word. Just one. Perhaps a few.
If only wishes could come true!

*

Next day I had a great idea.
The place to start became quite clear.
The word was one Bert often heard
and perfect for my noisy bird.
Perhaps you'd like to try to guess
the word that brought me such success?
Before your brain begins to hurt,
I'd better tell you. It was . . . "Bert".

Alphabetical Animals

Animals everywhere Always Amaze:
Big Beefy Buffaloes quietly graze;
Cats with their Claws out Can Climb and Can scratch;
Dogs Dive for balls using teeth for a catch;
Elephants' Ears are as big as can be;
Foxes From hunters can speedily Flee;
Gentle Giraffes are remarkably tall;
Heavyweight Hippos Have ears that are small.
I like the Ibex. It surely can climb.
Just don't wait for Zebra. I haven't the time!

Squirrel Sightings

Have you ever seen a squirrel?
You may think them rather cute,
But they're certainly not stupid,
for they're really quite astute.
They take notice of the weather
when the winter's on its way
And store all the food that's needed
for each coming frosty day.
For that is when they snuggle
in the hollow of a tree,
Or they hide among the bushes
where they're difficult to see.

Every squirrel's quite a builder
when it wants to make a nest,
So that as things get much colder
there's a place for warmth and rest.
If you should see a squirrel
when you're at the park to play,
Don't be too disappointed
if the squirrel darts away.
Watch him hurry, scamper, scurry,
for you'll seldom see him walk.
Perhaps he's just too busy
to take time to stop and talk.

GARDEN CREATURES

Rainbow's End

A snail once heard the story
Which is very often told:
"If you reach a rainbow's ending,
You will find a pot of gold!"
This idea was most appealing,
(Since the snail was very poor)
And it left him with a feeling
That he couldn't quite ignore.

Every day when it was raining,
But the clouds began to clear,
He would scan the sky for rainbows
In the hope one would appear.
Then at last he thought he saw one
In the garden hothouse glass!
To the spot he slowly hurried
Streaking silver through the grass.

But oh, what disappointment,
When he reached that special place!
For of golden coins or treasure,
He discovered not a trace.
As he turned to leave, discouraged,
Something caught his tearful eye
And a potted gold chrysanthemum
Proved the story was no lie.

Small Wonder

Please don't be frightened, sweet butterfly blue,
I just want to capture a picture of you.
As I inch closer I mean you no harm.
It's not my intention to cause you alarm.
Your wings are so delicate: colours so pretty!
Please don't fly away. That would be such a pity.
No need now to flutter, I'll keep this quite brief.
Just stay where you are on that rich deep green leaf.
That's perfect! I've got you! You'll soon be on show:
Your beauty shared proudly with people I know.

The Tortoise

The tortoise has a solid shell
And this protects it very well.
If frightened and it wants to hide
It tucks its head and legs inside.
Although its movement's rather slow
It still gets where it wants to go.
Despite its most ungainly gait
You'd never say it's running late!

"Supersnail"

I may not have a backbone,
But I'm brave as brave can be.
Just take time to observe me,
Then I'm sure you will agree.
My enemies are giants tall
And armed with hoes and spades!
They stomp around my picnic spots
And hurl their flashing blades!

Yet these will not deter me,
Since clearly I must eat
The greens left lying in my path:
How beautifully sweet!
I bravely dodge the missiles
And bomb-like boots from heights.
Such perils do not kill desire
To munch on such delights!

When climbing I am carefree:
Though high may be the wall,
I cling to ledges upside down
And never fear to fall.
So do not doubt my courage.
Admire my spiral shell!
Call me "a mighty mollusc"
And "Supersnail" as well!

The Happy Cricket

There was once a little cricket,
Who was happy as could be.
He was chirpy before breakfast.
He was chirpy after tea.
He was chirpy when the sun rose.
He was chirpy when it set.
When it comes to being chirpy,
No more chirpy could you get!

One time when he was chirping
As the sun came up at dawn,
He was hopping through the flowers;
He was jumping on the lawn;
But quite suddenly a sprinkler
Shot him with a shower of spray
And he didn't feel like chirping
Till the sprinkler went away.

Now this jolly little cricket
Really loved to have a dance,
He would look around for partners
When he ever had the chance.
Then they'd waltz around the kitchen;
And they'd jig right down the hall.
But they *really* kicked their heels up
At the weekly cricket ball!

*Accepted in 2017 for publication by the School Magazine

Who's Home?

You will find him in your garden
Yet he'll always be at home,
Which is strange, because he travels,
Though he never far will roam,
For his movement is quite sluggish
And he often stops to eat.
If you're growing nice green lettuce,
He considers that a treat!

With his eyes on stalks like flowers,
He can find his favourite food.
Never interrupt him eating,
Or he'll think you're very rude!
Do not fear that he'll attack you
As he cannot throw a punch;
He will just be feeling cranky
That you've spoiled his lovely lunch!

Since his home he carries with him,
He will never mind the rain
And if anything should scare him,
He just goes inside again!
You will look in vain for footprints
But you'll see his silver trail.
Do you think you know his name now . . . ?
Yes, you've got it! . . . Mr Snail!

FOOD & FAMILY

The Mystery Box

My lunch for school's a mystery box
and here's the reason why:
I cannot guess just what's inside,
however hard I try.
There's something different every day:
Mum treats it as a game.
The only thing I'm sure about:
no day will be the same.

If Monday's roll has vegemite,
then Tuesday's might have jam.
A sandwich made for Wednesday's lunch
might well be beef or ham.
On Thursday then, a salad wrap
could be the big surprise,
But one school lunch on Friday
something shocking met my eyes:

My mystery box was oozing
with a greenish-yellow trickle!
There must have been a mix-up
with Dad's favourite: cheese and pickle!
While Dad enjoyed my peanut paste
spread on his bread with honey,
My sandwich had an awful taste.
Don't laugh. It wasn't funny!

Sweet Treats

Here's a list of special treats
I'm sure you'd love to eat.
You might want to add some more
to make the list complete:

Marvellous marshmallows, yielding and chewy;
Soft-centred chocolates, so creamy and gooey;
Fabulous fairy floss, wispy and sticky,
(Keeping your face clean's especially tricky!);
Honeycomb crunchy and boiled lollies brittle:
None of this easy to stop at a little.

Yes, truly this sweet stuff is lovely to taste,
But too much is bound to add weight to your waist.
There's one further warning: I'll keep it quite brief.
Make sure that you never stop cleaning your teeth!

A Happiness Recipe

If you want to be happy
As happy can be,
Try not to keep asking
"What's in it for me?"
Enjoy what you have,
(Perhaps quite a lot)
And give far less thought
To what you have not.

Be happy you live,
Be happy you grow,
Be happy you learn
What many don't know,
Be happy to help
A person in need,
Be happy you're loved.
That's happy indeed!

Beating Eric's Eating

Young Eric was a little boy
who really loved to eat.
In any eating contest
he'd be very hard to beat.
His slender older sister
wouldn't ever be his match,
Nor did his bigger brother
think that Eric he could catch.
And even Eric's father,
who was more than average size,
When watching Eric eating
could not hide his great surprise,
For Eric's plate was piled up high
with food of every kind:
To see it quickly disappear
just blew his father's mind!

His mother's face looked anxious
as she eyed what Eric ate.
She thought: "If Eric keeps this up,
he'll put on too much weight.
I'll feed him lots of Brussels sprouts
and serve him tripe and brains.
That surely ought to put an end
to any weight he gains!"
But Eric didn't seem to mind;
he just kept eating faster;
He hardly tasted what he ate.
The plan was a disaster.
His father said: "This can't go on.
It's got beyond a joke.
If Eric keeps his eating up,
our family will go broke!"

They pondered for a moment,
thinking what next they could do.
His older sister said
that they should put him in a zoo!
"He'd only eat the animals",
replied his older brother.
"Enough of that! That's most unkind! "
responded Eric's mother.
"We have to think of something
that will make him want to stop,
Or else I'll spend hours every day
just going to the shop."
His desperate Dad was thinking fast:
"I think I know a way.
We'll start to ration all the food
we're going to eat each day."

"First, everyone will get a serve,
all generous, but the same.
When anybody asks for more,
then that will start the game.
You'll have to buy the extra food
you want put on your plate
And if you can't produce the cash,
food won't eventuate.
Your pocket money or your purse
could gain you new supplies,
But as your money disappears,
you soon will realise
There'll be no money left to buy
the things you want far more
And only empty pockets
will go with you to the store."

His Dad knew well that Eric
loved to spend his cash on sweets,
But money spent on extra food
meant none for special treats!
It was a most unhappy lad
who came to meals each day.
Instead of filling him with food,
they filled him with dismay.
His appetite began to wane.
He left scraps on the plate.
Before, with something left to eat,
he wouldn't hesitate.
The ration plan soon brought an end
to Eric's problem habit
And that is how his family
stopped him eating like a rabbit.

Sharing the Secret

Psst. Listen to this, Sis!

I'm going to whisper in your ear,
Because I don't want Dad to hear.
This secret's just come straight from Mum:
She's got a baby in her tum!
No-one must know, but you and me
And Mum, of course, but just we three.
I said to Mum I wouldn't tell,
So you must promise me as well,
Then when Dad hears the baby's cries,
He's going to get a huge surprise!

Tongue Torture

If you like to eat cold meat
and consider that a treat,
Have you ever thought of adding chilli sauce?
Use a little, not a lot,
since this sauce is rather hot
And you wouldn't want to singe your tongue, of course.

Don't be led astray by greed
and take more than you will need.
If you do, I can assure you,
you'll regret it.
Though your tongue may twist and turn,
your whole mouth will seem to burn
And I doubt you'll soon be able to forget it!

PEOPLE & PLACES

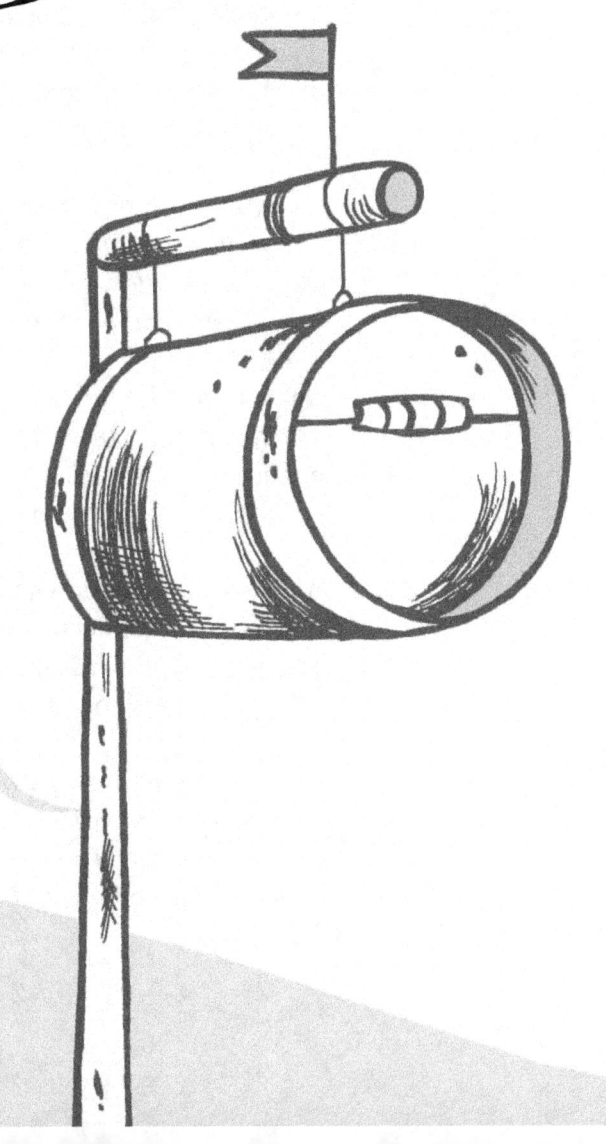

*The Mail Tin**

Way out west, where willows weep
By creek beds cracked and dry,
A mail tin stands atop a post
Beneath a cloudless sky.

The homestead sits behind a hill:
The mail tin far from view,
But there, round ten, a song is heard
And you may sing it too.

It's time to put the billy on.
It's time to fetch the mail!
It's time to catch a kangaroo
And swing it by its tail!

How is it that the farmer's wife
Can sing this silly song?
She sounds so sure the mail has come,
But what if she is wrong?

The farmhands stop, lay down their tools.
The youngest mounts his horse.
He rides away towards the road
To get the mail, of course!

It's time to put the billy on.
It's time to fetch the mail!
It's time to catch a kangaroo
And swing it by its tail!

The farmer's wife saw rising dust.
She heard the rumbling truck.
Her eyes and ears said: "There's the mail!"
It wasn't just good luck.

******

The years have passed. The mail tin's gone
That stood through heat and hail.
Not once they caught a kangaroo,
Nor swung it by its tail!

* Accepted in 2016 for publication by The School Magazine.

Beach Bottle

The bottle looked lost as it lay on the sand.
Perhaps it had fallen from somebody's hand.
It seemed to be empty, but still had its lid:
Whoever had dropped it must know that they did.
Or had it been lost from the deck of a boat,
With air trapped inside having helped it to float,
Until borne by the waves and washed up by the tide
It was left on the beach at the end of its ride?

Still, no one had claimed it. The bottle was mine!
It looked to have once held some cider or wine.
I bent down and grasped it, then held it up high
To check if inside it was thoroughly dry.
I found it not empty as first I had thought,
But rather, inside was a note of some sort!
I opened and read what was written within:
"Please take this old bottle and throw in the bin."

*Accepted in 2017 for publication by the School Magazine

My Ride to School

I'll ride my bike to school today:
I'm old enough and know the way.
From home my ride's towards the sun.
That's east, because day's just begun.
I find the sun gets in my eyes,
But at that time it's no surprise.

I ride east to an intersection.
Now it's time to change direction.
Left turn here's the way to go.
(Heading north, as you may know).
Right turn south would be quite wrong
And make my journey far too long!

I cross two roads with special care
And then I know I'm almost there.
My northward route curves left then right
To bring the school grounds into sight.
One last turn left - I'm through the gate!
I'm riding west and won't be late!

Pathway in the Park

The winter sun was sinking.
It was getting rather late.
Our parents would be waiting at
the park's main entrance gate.
"Make sure you're back by sunset!"
That had been Dad's final word,
But Mum chose to repeat it
to make sure that we had heard.

Because I was the oldest,
Dad had said I was in charge,
Adding: "Stay together always!"
since the park was very large.
Also quite important
was to stay close to the track,
For then we'd simply follow it
to make our way straight back.

We walked downhill some distance,
then we found a little creek.
This turned out really excellent
for playing hide and seek.
The trees and boulders by the banks
were great to hide behind
And in the creek some coloured stones,
I felt, were quite a find.

The time there passed more quickly
than I ever realised,
So when I glanced down at my watch,
I really was surprised.
"We've been here much too long!"
I cried, "It's time for us to go.
We can't afford to take our stones.
They'll make us far too slow."

The others tried to argue,
but I wouldn't change my mind.
The pathway back was steep uphill,
so stones were left behind.
We hid them underneath a bush
and hoped to come back soon
To find and play with them again,
some other afternoon.

The sun no longer warmed us
and we felt the winter chill.
The wind blew in our faces
as we climbed the steps uphill.
The shadows grew much longer
and the sky was turning red.
Our legs were getting weary,
but we faced more steps ahead.

Beyond the steps, in fading light,
our pathway took a bend
And as it curved off to the right
I thought we'd find the end,
But still the path continued on.
No gate came into view.
Nor was there sign of Mum or Dad.
What were we going to do?

The path was now all we had left
to guide us to the gate,
Since round us everything was dark
and we were awfully late.
The wind was whistling eerily:
a mournful sort of sound.
We huddled close together
and our hearts began to pound!

Just then I thought I heard a shout.
It sounded like my name.
"I'm here!" I cried with all my might.
The others did the same.
Despite the dark, we knew the voice,
it clearly was our Dad
And though we were in trouble,
I could not have been more glad!

Holiday Playground

Rambling round the ruins
Found in Greece and Rome,
We are merely tourists
Very far from home.
What it's like to live here
We can only guess.
Is it full of interest?
Hear us answer: "Yes"!

Ruins tell us stories
Of a nation's past,
But its former glories
Often do not last.
Wars and evil leaders
Good things can destroy;
Plagues and vile diseases
Steal a nation's joy.

Rambling round the ruins,
Climbing steps and stairs,
Weaving through the columns,
We cast off our cares.
Here we hide from siblings;
Trick our Dad and Mum;
Once we were reluctant.
Now we're glad we've come!

Clown Caper

Once a climbing clown,
Clambered up a tower,
Colander in hand,
Plus a cauliflower.
What he had in mind,
No-one seemed to know
And it wasn't clear,
How far up he'd go.

After quite a climb
He had reached the top,
Items still in hand,
He then let them drop!
Neither looked the same,
Fallen from the tower,
Not the colander,
Nor the cauliflower!

My Secret Place

Where can I find a secret place:
A place that's just for me,
Where I can go and no-one know,
Or looking, fail to see?

There none will tell me what to do,
Nor doubt that what I say is true.
Captain I'll be – without a crew,
There in my secret place!

Joys that I have, who then, will share?
Who'll cheer me up, when life's not fair?
Who, when I'm hurt, will quickly care,
There in my secret place?

Here's my new plan for what to do:
Search for a secret space for two!
No secret place that's just for one
Can have all I want to make it fun.

Buccaneer Secrets

When Spanish ships were making trips
To trade and gather treasure,
Crews learned to fear the buccaneer,
Whose boldness knew no measure.

I should be clear, a buccaneer
Was tough and rough and ruthless:
He'd climb aboard and use his sword
Or make his victims toothless.

Then, grabbing loot, he'd quickly scoot
Before someone could catch him.
He'd sail away to find more prey;
For daring, few could match him!

But now, today, I need to say
(Though sworn to keep it quiet):
He won't attack if there's a lack
Of fibre in his diet!

For I have heard, (it sounds absurd),
He craves a balanced meal,
Including beans and other greens
Before he'll sail to steal.

Don't think me wrong. I've heard the song
When buccaneers assemble.
They drop their 'g's, which does not please,
But these words make me tremble:

"Now bring your bunch of broccoli, boys
And throw it in the basin.
We'll eat it raw and call for more
Then ships we'll go a-chasin'!"

Colours of Courage

When I see both red and white,
I think about a fabled fight
That took place long ago.
A soldier brave rode out to save
A maiden from a dragon's cave.
That dragon was his foe!

With lance aloft and poised to pierce,
George rode toward that dragon fierce
And struck a lethal blow.
Then all at once its fiery breath,
Extinguished by its sudden death,
Was scarcely seen to glow!

The horse, once white, was quite a sight
With blood-red smears gained in the fight:
A most courageous steed!
Without his horse, St George, of course,
Would hardly be a fighting force
And likely, first to bleed!

In fighting flame, George made his name.
When victory came, he gained great fame.
"The man's a saint!" folk cried.
Now freed from fear and full of cheer,
They praised St George one day each year,
Long after he had died.

The story grew as stories do.
I fear that few may think it true.
I leave the verdict up to you.

*Beach Cones**

The shapes I like are conical.
They taper to the tip.
Perhaps you've seen some shells
like that when going for a dip.
Such shells are very pretty
and they're great fun to collect:
Their range of colours, streaks and spots
- much more than you'd expect!

While at the beach you may well see
a different kind of cone:
Far bigger, in a lifeguard's hand,
it's called a megaphone.
Through this his booming voice is heard
to call us back to shore.
It's warning us of danger
we'd be foolish to ignore.

When heading home, our swimming done,
one final cone I eat.
I'm sure you've guessed
just what it is, so icy cold and sweet!
Then as I lick the one I pick,
my tongue can taste and test.
Of all the cones I've ever known,
I like an ice-cream best!

** First published in The School Magazine:
Countdown, Feb. 2017*

My Tall Tower

One block, two blocks, three then four:
See my tower rise from the floor!
Five blocks, six blocks, seven, eight:
Make my building tall and straight!

Nine blocks, ten blocks, should I stop?
Two more blocks could be the top.
There, I've done it! Twelve blocks high!
One more block I'd like to try.

Take great care with block thirteen.
Whoops! My tower begins to lean!
Feel my heart start beating faster.
Trembling hands could cause disaster!

Block thirteen has left my hands.
Still my slanting structure stands!
Family, watching, start to clap.
Wake our dog up from his nap!

Spot begins to stretch and sniff,
Then of wood he gets a whiff.
Curious, he stops and blinks.
"Better check it out", he thinks.

Over to the tower he goes;
Pokes the bottom with his nose;
Tumbling blocks fall off the top;
Vain our cries, he doesn't stop.

Soon my tower's completely wrecked.
All the blocks I then collect.
One block, two blocks, three, then four:
Put the lot back in the drawer!

Bubble Trouble

I'll tell you the trouble with bubbles:
They burst like a punctured balloon
As they fall on a sharp piece of rubble,
Or they fail on their flight to the moon.
It's useless to try to collect them.
They're not like a coin or a stamp.
For the hand that you raise to protect them
You'll soon find is feeling quite damp.

Yet bubbles, you'd better believe it,
Can actually be lots of fun.
You can catch them and snatch them
And quickly despatch them
Until you have burst every one.
You can chase them all over your garden.
You can watch them drift over a wall.
Though you run like a hare,
As they're mostly just air,
When you search you'll find nothing at all!

Train Lines

If you dearly want to gain
A skill
Allow me to explain
The drill
You really have to train
Until
You can do it again
And again
At will.

Space Traveller

I plan to build a spaceship soon
and travel to the stars.
My Dad says: "Land first on the moon,
then buy more fuel on Mars."
But will the Martians sell me fuel
if I've no shopper docket?
I'll ask my Mum to give me one
and keep it in my pocket.

At school we learned the nearest star
is still quite far away.
This means the food I'll need to pack
must last more than one day.
So I should fit a cupboard in
where food can all be stored
And for my rest, it's surely best,
to put a bed on board.

My spaceship must have windows
where I'll watch the stars at night.
For sleeping, I'll make shutters
to keep out their dazzling light.
Since stars will be much closer
as I travel out in space,
There'd hardly be much sleeping
with them shining in my face!

I've worked it out. Without a doubt,
my spaceship will be large.
I ought to contact Fuel Watch too,
to learn what Martians charge.
I think perhaps I need more time.
There's so much I must do,
But once my spaceship's ready,
then I'll say goodbye to you.

Or would you like to help me build
and join me for the ride?
You needn't answer straight away,
there's still time to decide,
But if you plan to come along,
you too need food and bed.
So let's just ask our Mums
to take us to the zoo instead.

Accepted in 2017 for publication by the School Magazine

Seeking Stardom

There was a young man who once bought a guitar.
His goal was to strut on the stage as a star,
But when plucking a string,
It just broke with a "ping",
So he gave up and didn't get far.

Another young man bought a fine tennis racquet.
He dreamt of success that would make him a packet.
But his strokes were all wrong:
Balls he hit went too long.
When he saw any ball he'd just whack it!

A third wanted fame with a bat, playing cricket.
He went for a six, but fell onto his wicket!
"Owzat!?" came the shout.
Then the umpire cried: "Out!"
So, for fame then, the bat was no ticket.

Wally's Folly

My mate Wally had a collie
that he gave the name of Molly
And he thought it would be jolly
to pull Molly on a trolley,
But poor Molly, when she tried it,
was determined not to ride it,
So that once it hit a bump,
she decided she would jump.

Now when Molly left the trolley
she soon showed me Wally's folly,
For without the weight of Molly
even faster went the trolley
And while Wally tried to race it,
he was failing to outpace it,
So it quickly knocked him over,
but with luck he fell on clover.

Soon he had a lick from Molly,
who felt sorry for poor Wally,
But both Wally and his collie
just ignored the upturned trolley,
Then with Wally's heels near bleeding
and the collie always leading,
They went back to where they started
and much wiser I departed.

Rubik Remembered

Once a clever man named Rubik
Made a puzzle that was cubic.
Lots of people went to buy it:
Some just couldn't wait to try it.

All six faces full of colour,
Made the other toys look duller!
Red and yellow, blue and green,
Orange, white could all be seen.

Every face's shape was square,
Cubes are like that everywhere.
Length and width and height the same:
Like the dice used in a game.

Nine small squares on every face,
In each large square had a place.
These could twist in groups of threes
To a different face with ease.

Here is what you had to do:
Make one face completely blue,
Or perhaps choose green or red,
Orange, yellow, white, instead.

Then the rest, till one by one,
Every single colour done!
Few could do it. Most could not.
I was in that second lot.

WEATHER WATCHING

Stop, rain, stop!

Stop, rain, stop!
Not another drop!
My friends are here. They've come to play.
We want to be outdoors today.
Stop, rain, stop!

Stop, rain, stop!
Not another drop!
We do not want our washing wet,
But you make sure that's what we get.
Stop, rain, stop!

Stop, rain, stop!
Not another drop!
You've been around for several hours:
Look how you're drowning all the flowers!
Stop, rain, stop!

Stop, rain, stop!
Not another drop!
Go help the farmer grow his wheat
And give his stock green grass to eat.
Stop, rain, stop!

Drip . . . . . drip . . . . plop!
At last, the final drop!
Now we'll get a flower display.
Now the washing's on its way.
Now we can go out to play!

Winter: A Child's Guide

When the wind howls through the trees;
When you fear your feet will freeze;
When dark clouds obscure the sun;
Know that winter has begun.

Now's the time the days seem short;
Now a cold can soon be caught;
Now more frequent rain will fall;
It's just winter - that is all.

Thunderstorms may come and go;
On high mountains there'll be snow;
Frost may form upon the grass:
This is winter. It will pass.

Winter's time for active play.
Grab your gear without delay!
Put your boots on! Join your team!
Soon much warmer it will seem!

If you'd rather play inside,
Indoor games wait to be tried.
With your family or a friend,
Boredom soon will quickly end.

Start a hobby and collect.
Fix a toy that someone wrecked.
Solve a puzzle. Draw or paint.
Clean your room. Your Mum will faint!

Drink hot chocolate by the fire.
Read an author you admire.
Whether you're a girl or boy,
Don't miss out on winter joy!

Winter Picnic

One picnic with my family
I would rather now forget,
Since it started with a thunderstorm
that left us very wet.
We ran like rabbits to the car
and tried to eat our lunch,
But our sandwiches were soggy
and our biscuits lacked their crunch.

We aimed to keep the rain out
so we wound the windows up,
But that just made them foggy.
Then I dropped my half-full cup!
My parents weren't too pleased with me
as anyone could tell
And then the baby filled the car
with a most awful smell!

At last we saw the rain had stopped,
so quickly we got out.
Mum changed the baby's nappy.
It was then Dad gave a shout.
"Oh no, we've run over a nail!"
He'd found a tyre was flat.
So we weren't going anywhere
till he had dealt with that.

While Dad was working on the wheel,
I got my brand new ball.
I kicked it high into a tree,
but it refused to fall!
So then I said: "I'll climb the tree
and shake the football down."
But Mum said: "You'll do no such thing"
and stopped me with a frown.

I didn't want to lose the ball,
but what would you have done?
It looked as if I'd have to save
to buy another one.
Just then a teenage boy came by.
He said: "Leave it to me."
At once he climbed up to the
branch and shook the football free!

I tried to catch it as it fell,
but Mum caught it instead.
She didn't catch it in her hands.
It landed on her head!
I thought it wasn't wise to laugh
in case she was upset.
She'd told me not to bring the ball.
I hoped that she'd forget.

When finally Dad changed the tyre,
he said: "It's time to go.
Those heavy clouds are coming back.
The journey will be slow."
I moaned: "An hour here's not enough.
We need some time to play!"
But Mum declared: "Your Dad is right.
Let's come another day."

Although this time our picnic
didn't seem much fun at all,
We did arrive home safely
and I still had my new ball.
The baby now is chuckling
and we're by the fire and warm.
It still was an adventure,
even with the winter storm.

Sometimes . . .

Sometimes in the sunshine,
Sometimes in the shade;
Hiking through a forest,
Marching on parade;
Sometimes seeking shelter,
When the sun is hot;
Sometimes craving sunshine,
When the weather's not.

Sometimes we are wanting
Warmth upon our skin;
Other times we're wearing
What can keep warmth in.
When the weather changes,
We start changing too.
So it seems the weather
Tells us what to do!

*T is for TROUBLE**

T's always starting Trouble
as we very clearly see,
In Trains it must sit at the front,
as selfish as can be,
Then when it comes to Taking Turns,
of course it must be first,
As Time and Time again,
in this, it really is the worst.

Its influence is very bad,
of that there is no doubt,
For when there's work for it to do
we find it backing ouT.
A man named Ben was joined by T
and instantly was BenT,
So gained a reputation
that was never his intent!

Now people sometimes tell you,
you should "mind your Ps and Qs",
But when it comes to letters
there's another that I'd choose.
Its awfully bad behaviour's bound
to lead you into error,
So I'd advise: "Beware of T!"
It truly is a Terror.

*Accepted in 2016 for publication by
The School Magazine.*

Party Preparation

I say to my mirror: "Well, how do I look?"
The mirror replies: "You use your two eyes."
"No, you don't understand! Tell me how I appear."
"You come through the door and then you are here."
"But mirror of mine, tell me what you reflect."
"Whatever's in front of me, as you'd expect."
"So, mirror of mine, have you no more to say?"
"Only: 'Why stand and stare? You've a party today!'"

Ready to Rhyme

I find when I am writing,
I oft resort to rhyme.
I don't know why I do it.
It happens all the time.
But if you like my writing,
(I really hope you will),
You'll find that I'll keep writing
In rhyming verses still!

*Wacky Words**

Perhaps you thought a pillar
was a man who swallowed pills,
Which had flavours like vanilla
and were meant to cure his ills,
But no pillars will be sickly,
for they're strong and stout and tall.
They are there to hold the roof up
and without them it would fall.

Perhaps you thought a meddler
was a man who went to war
And then came back home with medals
that he didn't wear before,
But most meddlers are a nuisance,
for they like to interfere,
So that when they finish meddling,
then their victims give a cheer!

Perhaps you thought a pedlar
would be one to ride a bike,
Pushing pedals from its saddle
with no wish to drive or hike,
But while pedlars can be mobile,
for they have their wares to sell,
They may spread their goods on pavement
and walk to your door as well.

It's true, some words we read
in books can give the wrong idea,
But using helpful dictionaries
can make their meanings clear.
Now no pillars, pedlars, meddlers,
should be leaving you perplexed,
So I wonder what the word
will be you'll want to look up next!?

* Accepted in June 2017 for publication by The School Magazine.

A Reason to Rhyme

Must our poems rhyme
ALL the time?
No. Not so.
Don't you know
Some verse is free
Like a fish in the sea?
But personally, I prefer my fish
Served on a regular dish
(With chips).

Acknowledgements

The author gratefully acknowledges the professional guidance of Karen McDermott of Making Magic Happen and gifted illustrator Veronica Rooke during the publishing process.

I am also indebted to Teena Raffa-Mulligan for her foreword. Her prompts on australianchildrenspoetry.com.au started me on the journey to publication. Her encouraging feedback, along with that of other users of the site, has propelled me forward.

To Teena, Pat Simmons and Janeen Brian, all themselves accomplished writers, I say a big "thank you" for their willingness to assist potential purchasers of this book with their impressions of my work.

Finally, I would like to thank my wife, Sheena, for the personal sacrifices and helpful suggestions she has made during the time this book has been in preparation.

About the author

Monty Edwards has been writing light-hearted rhyming verse for family birthdays, weddings and other special occasions for many years, as well as exploring Christian themes in his "Poems on the Way". His early experience as a primary school teacher and now as a grandparent has resulted in a new focus on writing for children, to growing acclaim.

Monty lives in beachside Rockingham, south of Perth, Western Australia.
He has dedicated The Mystery Box to
his five much-loved grandchildren.

Tia, Saraya & Duke; Zoe & Siena.

www.ingramcontent.com/pod-product-compliance
Lightning Source LLC
Chambersburg PA
CBHW072109290426
44110CB00014B/1877